1863: THE CRUCIAL YEAR

A SOURCEBOOK ON THE CIVIL WAR

1863: THE CRUCIAL YEAR

A SOURCEBOOK ON THE CIVIL WAR

Edited by Carter Smith

AMERICAN ALBUMS FROM THE COLLECTIONS OF
THE LIBRARY OF CONGRESS

THE MILLBROOK PRESS, *Brookfield, Connecticut*

Cover: "Storming Fort Wagner." Lithograph by Kurz & Allison, nineteenth century.

Title Page: View from the summit of Little Round Top at the Battle of Gettysburg. Oil painting by Edwin Forbes.

Contents Page: "Rally Round the Flag Boys: Victory at Last." Lithograph by Currier & Ives, 1861.

Back Cover: " Battle of Port Hudson." Lithograph by L. Prang & Co., 1863.

Library of Congress Cataloging-in-Publication Data

1863 : the crucial year : a sourcebook on the Civil War / edited by Carter Smith.
 p. cm. — (American albums from the collections of the Library of Congress)
  Includes bibliographical references and index.
  Summary: Uses a variety of contemporary materials to describe and illustrate certain key events of the Civil War that took place during 1863.
  ISBN 1-56294-263-8 (lib. bdg.)
  1. United States—History—Civil War, 1861–1865—Juvenile literature. 2. United States—History—Civil War, 1861–1865—Pictorial works—Juvenile literature. 3. United States—History—Civil War, 1861–1865—Sources—Juvenile literature. [1. United States—History—Civil War, 1861–1865—Sources.] I. Smith, C. Carter. II. Series.
E468.A123 1993
973.7'34'0222—dc20   92-16547
                                                                          CIP
                                                                          AC

 Created in association with Media Projects Incorporated

C. Carter Smith, *Executive Editor*
Lelia Wardwell, *Managing Editor*
Charles A. Wills, *Principal Writer*
Kimberly Horstman, *Picture and Production Editor*
Lydia Link, *Designer*
Athena Angelos, *Photo Researcher*

The consultation of Bernard F. Reilly, Jr., Head Curator of the Prints and Photographs Division of the Library of Congress, is gratefully acknowledged.

10 9 8 7 6 5 4 3 2 1

256 79939

Contents

A SHORT HISTORY OF

GEN. R.E. LEE.

General Robert E. Lee masterminded one of the South's greatest victories—the Battle of Chancellorsville—and presided over one of its worst defeats—the Battle of Gettysburg—in 1863. This portrait comes from a series of trading cards included in packets of Duke cigarettes around 1900.

Introduction

1863: THE CRUCIAL YEAR is one of the volumes in a series published by The Millbrook Press titled AMERICAN ALBUMS FROM THE COLLECTIONS OF THE LIBRARY OF CONGRESS, and one of six books in the series subtitled SOURCEBOOKS ON THE CIVIL WAR.

The editors' basic goal for the series is to make available to the student many of the original visual documents preserved in the Library of Congress as records of the American past. The volumes in THE CIVIL WAR series reproduce prints, broadsides, maps, paintings, and other works from the Library's special collections divisions, and a few from its general book collections. Most prominently featured in this series are the holdings of the Prints and Photographs Division.

The pivotal events of 1863 were recorded and reported to the home front in a multitude of prints, drawings, and photographs. The many decisive and costly military encounters of the year generated a flood of battle prints by publishers such as Currier & Ives, Sarony and Major, and others. The Library of Congress possesses the most comprehensive archive of these prints, including almost all of Currier & Ives's known Civil War prints. The artist-reporters dispatched to the field by the major newspapers and magazines of the period were especially productive during 1863. As this and the other volumes in this series show, the Library's Civil War archives are particularly rich in field drawings done by Alfred Waud and Edwin Forbes

in 1863, including an extensive series of paintings by Forbes of Gettysburg.

The many kinds of pictorial records that survive invite our comparison. How events were portrayed differs substantially between the battle prints produced for public sale in the North, the field drawings done for magazines and newspapers, and the portrayals of Civil War battles produced by Kurz & Allison and other publishers after the war. The first were idealized to glorify the Union cause. The field drawings were far more realistic and rough (and were consequently often modified by newspaper editors before publication). Artists painting and drawing these scenes later in the century, on the other hand, invested them with a spirit of adventure imaginable only after the immediate horrors of the conflict had passed.

The photographic record of the war is also worthy of close appraisal. The fascinating "botched" photograph of Lincoln during his Gettysburg Address (page 77) speaks volumes about the occasion and the times—of the interest of the onlookers in the camera rather than the speaker, and the photographer's haste due to the unexpected brevity of Lincoln's speech.

The documents reproduced here represent a small but telling portion of the rich pictorial record of the Civil War preserved by the Library of Congress in its role as the nation's library.

BERNARD F. REILLY, JR.

The Civil War was fought over a vast area. The great distances involved created benefits and disadvantages for both sides. The Confederacy had a huge territory to defend, and Union troops could invade at any number of points. By 1863, Northern forces had penetrated into the Confederacy from Florida to Texas, and from Virginia to Louisiana. But the Union's successes in 1863, especially in the Mississippi River Valley, actually weakened Northern military strength in some ways. As Union troops advanced farther into the South, more and more soldiers had to be left behind to occupy unfriendly territory and to protect supply lines and bases from pro-Southern guerrillas and Confederate cavalry raiders. This helped to narrow the gap between the Union and Confederate armies' fighting strength.

Geography also played a major role in campaigns. The Union's many attempts to capture Richmond were frustrated, in part, because rivers such as the Rapidan and Rappahannock ran from west to east. Thus, Union forces moving south from around Washington toward the Confederate capital had to make river crossings—not an easy task for a large, cumbersome fighting force such as the Army of the Potomac. The Confederate Army of Northern Virginia faced only one major natural obstacle, the Potomac River, when it began its second invasion of the North in July 1863. The fact that the Allegheny and Blue Ridge mountains ran from north to south helped the Confederacy, because these ranges screened Southern troop movements from Northern observation.

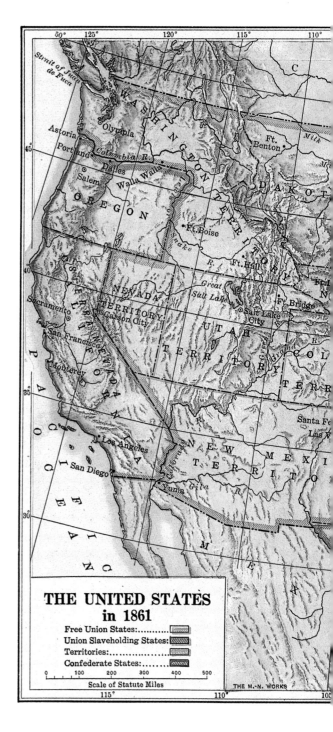

THE UNITED STATES in 1861

Free Union States:..........
Union Slaveholding States:
Territories:..............
Confederate States:.......

0   100   200   300   400   500
Scale of Statute Miles

THE M.-N. WORKS

9

A TIMELINE OF MAJOR EVENTS
January 1863–April 1863

AT HOME AND ABROAD

January 1, 1863 The Emancipation Proclamation becomes law. Although the decree does not order the immediate release of all slaves, it officially makes the abolition of slavery one of the Union's war goals.
•The Union's Emancipation Proclamation meets with anger in the Confederacy; a leading Richmond newspaper calls it a "startling political crime."

January 27 A. D. Boileau is arrested in Philadelphia for publishing anti-Union articles. Boileau is one of many Northern journalists and politicians arrested for spreading "disloyal sentiments."

February 1 Inflation reduces the value of Confederate currency to about 20 cents per Union dollar.

February 2 Congress authorizes free distribution of tobacco seeds to Northern farmers, in order to weaken the South's economy (which depends on tobacco as well as cotton) by competition.

February 5 Queen Victoria announces that the British government will not offer to negotiate a settlement in the American Civil War. In the wake of the Emancipation Proclamation, however, the British government and the British public are increasingly pro-Union.

February 6 After meeting with French diplomats, Union secretary of state William Seward declines their proposal to negotiate a peace treaty between the Union and the Confederacy.

February 26 The Cherokee Indian Nation rejoins the Union. The nation's council had voted to ally itself with the Confederacy in 1861.

MILITARY EVENTS

January 1, 1863 "Cottonclads" (improvised Confederate warships) capture one Union blockade vessel and sink another in the harbor at Galveston, Texas.
•General Ambrose Burnside resigns as commander of the Army of the Potomac, but President Lincoln persuades him to keep his post.

January 2–18 Several Union gunboats advance past Confederate battle positions at Vicksburg, Mississippi, although two are later captured.

January 3 The four-day battle at Murfreesboro in Tennessee finally ends when Braxton Bragg's Confederate troops withdraw from the area. Though victorious, Union forces have suffered heavily.

January 19–22 The Army of the Potomac again moves toward Fredericksburg, Virginia, but rain turns the advance into a brutal trek the soldiers call the "Mud March."

January 26 Secretary of War Edwin Stanton authorizes the recruitment of black troops for the Union armies. Two Union regiments, the 54th and 55th, have already formed in the state of Massachusetts.

The "Mud March"

March 3 To finance the war, Congress passes a law that authorizes the treasury to issue paper money.

•Faced with declining enlistments and a manpower shortage, Congress passes a law authorizing conscription. The law is full of loopholes, including one which allows the wealthy to avoid the draft either by paying a fee or by hiring a substitute.

March 13 An explosion at a Confed-

erate munitions plant near Richmond leaves sixty-nine workers dead or injured, almost all of them women.

March 26 West Virginia votes to free all its slaves.

April 1 Three thousand people, mostly women, riot in Richmond because of the high price and scarcity of food brought on by the Union blockade.

April 10 Worried by the South's lack of economic

Paper money issued by the Union

self-sufficiency, President Jefferson Davis urges Southern planters to give up growing cotton and tobacco and to concentrate on corn and other food crops.

April 24 The Confederate Congress

authorizes new taxes to pay for the war effort. The most controversial measure is a "tax in kind," which requires planters and farmers to set aside 10 percent of their crops and animals for government use.

January 29 Following the disastrous Mud March, Burnside is transferred to the Western Theater and General Joseph Hooker takes over command of the Army of the Potomac.

March 10 In order to stop desertions in the Union Army, President Lincoln issues a proclamation stating that deserters who return to duty by April 1 will not be punished. Punishment for desertion was often death by

firing squad in both the Union and Confederate armies.

March 14 Union warships launch an unsuccessful attack on the Mississippi River stronghold of Port Hudson, Louisiana.

April 7 A Union fleet attacks Charleston, South Carolina, but the operation fails after fierce fire from the many Confederate forts along the harbor forces the Union ships to withdraw.

April 15 The Confederate commerce raider *Alabama* sinks two Northern whaling ships in the South Atlantic. The *Alabama* is one of several Confederate warships searching the seas for Union ships in order to capture and destroy valuable cargo.

April 16 Union warships make it past Confederate positions at Vicksburg, giving the Union added firepower on the upper Mississippi River.

April 30 The Army of the Potomac crosses the Rappahannock and Rapidan rivers in yet another advance on Fredericksburg, Virginia.

•After several failed attempts to capture or bypass Vicksburg on the Louisiana side of the Mississippi River, Grant's troops land on the eastern bank of the river in the state of Mississippi.

A TIMELINE OF MAJOR EVENTS
May 1863–July 1863

AT HOME AND ABROAD

May 3 Roman Catholic Members of the Knights of the Golden Circle—a pro-Confederate secret society operating in Iowa, Ohio, and other midwestern states—are threatened with excommunication by their bishops.

May 5 Clement Vallandigham is arrested in Ohio for publicly protesting the war; he is tried for treason and sentenced to prison, although the sentence is later changed to banishment from the Union. Vallandigham becomes a hero for the North's "Copperheads."

May 11 Responding to criticism, Union treasury secretary Salmon Chase offers his resignation to President Lincoln for a second time. Again, Lincoln refuses to accept it.

June Panic spreads through the Union as General Lee advances into Pennsylvania; merchants in communities as far north as Philadelphia and New York City shut their shops and flee to the countryside.

June 8 President Lincoln proclaims that all immigrants in the North who intend to become citizens are liable to be drafted into the Union Army.

June 11 "Peace Democrats" in Ohio nominate Clement

Immigrant returning to Ireland to avoid the draft

Vallandigham for governor, despite the fact that he has been banished from the Union by President Lincoln.

MILITARY EVENTS

May 1 The Confederate Congress announces that black Union soldiers who are captured will be executed or, if they are fugitive slaves, returned to their owners.

May 4 The four-day Battle of Chancellorsville ends when the Army of the Potomac retreats back across the Rappahannock River. The brilliant Southern victory is marred when Stonewall Jackson is accidentally wounded by his own troops; he dies six days later.

May 12–17 In a series of battles in Mississippi, General Grant defeats Confederate forces under generals John Pemberton and Joseph E. Johnston. It is the final phase of the campaign for Vicksburg.

June 9 Confederate general J.E.B. Stuart's troopers clash with Union horsemen at Brandy Station, Virginia, in the largest cavalry battle of the war. The conflict ends in a draw.

July 1 A Confederate patrol enters Gettysburg, Pennsylvania, in search of shoes for the troops. A skirmish with Union cavalry grows into a full-scale battle as Union general George Meade rushes reinforcements into the area.

July 2 The Battle of Gettysburg continues as Lee's Confederates try, unsuccessfully, to drive Union forces from their positions on the high ground around the town.

July 3 The third day of fighting at Gettysburg climaxes in an unsuccessful 15,000-man Confederate assault on the Union positions. (The attack is quickly dubbed "Pickett's Charge," although General George Pickett's

June 12 Confederate vice president Alexander Stephens suggests to Jefferson Davis that the North and South work toward "a correct understanding and agreement between the two governments."

June 20 West Virginia officially becomes the thirty-fifth state.

June 29 In perhaps the largest mass escape during the war, 6,000 slaves (along with nearly 5,000 mules, horses, and cattle) safely reach Union lines in Louisiana.

July 1 Missouri abolishes slavery within its borders.

July 13 Anger with the federal draft law explodes into

Alexander Stephens

bloody rioting in New York City. The rioters, mostly Irish immigrants, turn their fury against the city's blacks, whom they believe are responsible for the war.

July 16 The New York draft riots end when Union troops arrive from Gettysburg to restore order. Over 1,000 people have been killed or injured, most of them blacks.

July 17 Horatio Seymour, Democratic governor of New York, makes a controversial speech urging peace with the South. His remarks (as well as his opposition to the Emancipation Proclamation) lead to severe criticism from Northern politicians and the press.

July 20 A group of New York businessmen set up a fund to aid blacks injured or made homeless by the draft riots.

troops make up only part of the force involved.)
•Cut off from help and suffering the effects of a six-week-long siege, the Confederate garrison at Vicksburg prepares to surrender the city to Union forces.

July 4 Lee's army begins its retreat from Gettysburg; rain, combined with slowness on Meade's part, allows the defeated Confederates to escape southward.
•Pemberton surren-ders Vicksburg to Grant, giving the Union almost complete control of the Mississippi River. The twin victories at Gettysburg and Vicksburg turn the tide of the war in the Union's favor.

July 9 Port Hudson, Louisiana, the last Mississippi River port in Confederate hands, surrenders to Union general Nathaniel Banks. The Mississippi is now completely under Union control.

July 12 Lee's army crosses the Potomac River to safety in Confederate-held territory.

July 18 Union troops launch an assault on Fort Wagner outside Charleston, South Carolina, and are beaten back with heavy losses. In the forefront of the attack is the 54th Massachusetts regiment, made up of black soldiers.

Attack of Johnston's division on Culp's Hill at the Battle of Gettysburg

AT HOME AND ABROAD

August 18 Kit Carson, a famous Western scout and now a colonel in the Union Army, begins a campaign against Navajo Indians in the Arizona Territory.
•President Lincoln personally test-fires a new gun model manufactured for use by Union cavalry.

September 3 In revenge for the Sioux uprising of 1862, General Alfred Sully leads an attack on an Indian village in the Dakota Territory, killing over 200 Indians—including many women and children—and taking 200 more prisoner.

September 4 Due to worsening economic conditions in the Confederacy, a bread riot breaks out in Mobile, Alabama. Troops are called in to break up the mob, but they refuse to fire on the crowd.

Kit Carson and the trappers in camp

September 5 In response to protests from Washington, the British government seizes two Confederate warships being built in a Liverpool shipyard. Until now, most of the Confederacy's oceangoing warships have been constructed in British ports.

October 3 President Lincoln declares a

MILITARY EVENTS

August 16 Union general William Rosecrans begins an advance on the strategic city of Chattanooga, Tennessee, on the opening day of the Chickamauga Campaign.

August 20 Confederate "irregulars" (guerrillas), led by Colonel William Quantrill, attack Lawrence, Kansas. The town is practically destroyed and almost 200 people are killed.

September 6 General Braxton Bragg's Confederate troops abandon Chattanooga,

The Battle of Chickamauga

Tennessee, as General Rosecrans's Union troops approach. Bragg hopes to trap the Union forces outside the city.

September 19 Skirmishes along Chickamauga Creek, Tennessee, develop into a conflict that will become the bloodiest clash in the Western part of the war.

September 20 Confederate troops under Braxton Bragg attack and scatter much of Rosecrans's force as the Battle of Chickamauga continues. Troops under General George Thomas hold off the Confederate assault,

day of Thanksgiving in the Union to commemorate the victories at Vicksburg and Gettysburg.

October 17 President Lincoln authorizes the enlistment of 300,000 men, by recruitment or draft, for three years or the duration of the war.

November 10 British diplomats inform Lincoln of a Confederate plot to raid Johnson's Island, a Union prison on

Lake Erie, and free the Confederates.

Abraham Lincoln

November 19 After a two-hour speech by famous orator Edwin Everett, President Lincoln delivers a "few words" at the dedication of the National Cemetery at Gettysburg. Although disregarded at the time, Lincoln's Gettysburg Address is later considered a masterpiece.

December The huge dome over the Capitol building in Washington, D.C., is lowered into place. President

Lincoln had ordered that work on the dome continue as a symbol of his faith that the nation would be reunited.

December 8 Looking toward the end of the war, President Lincoln offers amnesty to Confederates who agree to free their slaves and take an oath of loyalty to the United States.

---

allowing the rest of the Union Army to retreat.

September 21–22 Bragg's army fails to pursue Union forces as they retreat into Chattanooga. The Confederates take up positions on nearby Lookout Mountain and Missionary Ridge.

October 23 General Grant takes command of the Union forces under siege in Chattanooga. Grant's first task is to organize a

supply line, called the "cracker line," to keep his troops from starving.

November 24 The Battle of Chattanooga begins with a Union victory, as troops under General Joseph Hooker force the Confederates from the high ground of Lookout Mountain.

November 25 The Battle of Chattanooga continues with another successful Union assault, this time on Missionary

Ridge. Bragg's army retreats into Georgia.

John Hunt Morgan

November 28 Confederate general John Hunt Morgan and six of his men escape from the Ohio State Penitentiary by digging their way out with knives and spoons. (He was imprisoned for leading raids through the Union states of Kentucky, Ohio, and Indiana the previous year.)

Part I
High Tide for the Confederacy

In 1863, there were several major cavalry raids in both the Eastern and Western theaters of the war. One took place between April 29 and May 8, when General George Stoneman led the Army of the Potomac's cavalry on a ride deep into Virginia in order to divert the Confederate cavalry and to disrupt General Lee's communication with Richmond. Although Stoneman's cavalry reached the outskirts of the Confederate capital, the raid had little real military value. Also, Stoneman's absence during the Battle of Chancellorsville, fought while the raid was in progress, left Union general Joseph Hooker without reliable intelligence about Confederate troop movements.

At the start of 1863, the North's military successes were at a low point. The Army of the Cumberland was in the middle of a brutal three-day battle at Murfreesboro, Tennessee, on New Year's Day. Farther west, Ulysses S. Grant's campaign against Vicksburg, the Confederacy's Mississippi River stronghold, had stalled. In the East, the Army of the Potomac, still recovering from a bitter defeat at Fredericksburg, prepared to begin yet another ill-fated advance against Richmond.

But the Emancipation Proclamation brought a new sense of purpose to the North, stiffening its war effort. This document, first issued after the Battle of Antietam in September 1862, made freedom for the slaves a new Union goal. From this point on, both sides realized that a peace based on compromise would be impossible.

The first half of 1863 marked the high tide of the Confederacy. Jefferson Davis, unlike Abraham Lincoln, had found a general who could bring him victories: Robert E. Lee. When the Army of the Potomac began to move through Virginia again in the spring, Lee was ready. He and his army scored a brilliant victory at the Battle of Chancellorsville—a triumph made tragic by the death of Stonewall Jackson.

After Chancellorsville, Lee's Army of Northern Virginia seemed invincible to many people in both the North and the South. As summer approached, Lee and Davis planned the South's boldest move—an invasion of the North. In June Lee's army left Virginia, with the Army of the Potomac in pursuit. As July 1863 began, the two great armies met, almost accidentally, at a small Pennsylvania town called Gettysburg.

THE EMANCIPATION PROCLAMATION

The road to emancipation was gradual. At the start of the war, many people in the North had believed that secession, not slavery, was the chief issue of the conflict. Although he hated slavery, Lincoln at first shared this sentiment. "If I could save the Union without freeing any slave, I would do it; and if I could save it by freeing all the slaves, I would do it; and if I could save it by freeing some and leaving others alone, I would also do that," he had written.

As the war dragged on, however, Lincoln's feelings changed. On July 22, 1862, he told his cabinet that he intended to outlaw slavery in the Confederate states unless they ended their rebellion. Secretary of State William Seward urged Lincoln to delay the announcement of his plan until Union forces had won a significant victory. So Lincoln waited until September 22—just after the Battle of Antietam—to make public his "Preliminary Emancipation Proclamation." It gave the Confederate states until January 1, 1863, to return to the Union. When they did not, the Emancipation Proclamation became law. Under its terms, Lincoln declared that all slaves in areas "in rebellion against the United States . . . shall be . . . forever free." From now on, the North was fighting not just to restore the Union, but also to free the slaves.

This fanciful painting of Lincoln (opposite, top) drafting the Emancipation Proclamation is filled with symbols of secession, slavery, and conflict. These include copies of speeches by John C. Calhoun and Daniel Webster, a map of Europe hung next to a sword, and a bust of Andrew Jackson. The tired look on the president's face, however, reflects reality. In July 1862, Lincoln told Secretary of the Navy Gideon Welles that the question of emancipation "occupies my mind and thoughts day and night."

Lincoln is reading an early draft of the Emancipation Proclamation to his cabinet in this painting (right). Secretary of State William Seward told Lincoln to set the document aside "until you can give it to the country supported by military success." Seward warned that otherwise it might be seen as "the last measure of an exhausted government, a cry for help . . . our last shriek on the retreat."

THE NORTH REACTS TO EMANCIPATION

The Emancipation Proclamation met with mixed reactions. Some people pointed out that the document didn't free a single slave, since it could not take effect until the South was conquered. Also, the law did not address slavery in border slave states that had stayed in the Union.

Others hailed the law as a giant step toward freedom for all American blacks. "We shout for joy that we live to recall this moment," said Frederick Douglass. William Lloyd Garrison called the proclamation "a great historic event, sublime in its magnitude, momentous . . . in its far-reaching consequences."

Emancipation also had practical benefits. Slaves were one of the South's economic resources. Freeing them would deprive the Confederacy of much of its labor force. "Every slave withdrawn from the enemy," said Union general in chief Henry Halleck, "is the equivalent of a white man *hors de combat* [out of action]." In order to free the slaves, however, the Union would need to move even farther into the South.

The proclamation had an immediate impact on foreign affairs. Since no European nation wanted to appear to support slavery, the document subdued pro-Confederate feeling in Britain and France. Charles Francis Adams, the U.S. minister in London, wrote, "the Emancipation Proclamation has done more for us here than all our former victories and all our diplomacy."

This elaborate print was one of many issued in the North to celebrate the Emancipation Proclamation. The text lists the Confederate states where the proclamation applied; however, some Union-occupied parts of Virginia, Louisiana, and Tennessee were exempted from emancipation. Surrounding the Proclamation are scenes of what many people thought the slaves could expect after emancipation: education, fair wages, and the freedom to worship.

THE BATTLE OF MURFREESBORO

In late 1862, General William S. Rosecrans had replaced Don Carlos Buell as commander of the Army of the Cumberland. On December 26, Rosecrans led a force of 45,000 men south from Nashville, Tennessee. Their goal was Stones River, next to the town of Murfreesboro, where Braxton Bragg and 37,000 Confederate soldiers were camped.

Rosecrans divided his forces into left and right wings. The left wing was to hold the Confederates in place while the right wing attacked. Bragg was planning to do the very same with his forces, however.

But the Battle of Murfreesboro (called the Battle of Stones River in the South) didn't go according to plan. On December 31, a bitterly cold day, Bragg struck Rosecrans first, and with such force that the Union troops could not maneuver. They could only try to hold their positions as Confederates swept across the frozen battlefield, shouting. Thousands of Northern soldiers fled. But one corps, led by General George Thomas—a Virginian who had remained loyal to the Union—stood fast. Thanks to Thomas and other determined Union officers and soldiers, the Northerners were still on the field as night fell.

Exhausted after the fierce fighting on December 31, Union general George Thomas (1816–70; above) fell asleep as Rosecrans and his staff debated about whether to break off the fight at Murfreesboro. When somebody said the word "retreat," Thomas awoke instantly. He said, "This army can't retreat!" and went back to sleep. At Chickamauga, in November, Thomas would once again refuse to yield his ground to a massive Confederate assault.

The superiority of General Rosecrans's artillery was one of the factors that led Confederate general Braxton Bragg (1817–76) to halt Confederate assaults on January 2. One Union officer said that the artillery "saved the army" at Murfreesboro. This gun crew (right) was part of the Union force that advanced on Murfreesboro as 1862 ended.

General William Rosecrans (1819–98; right), "Old Rosey" to his soldiers, was a big, hearty man whose style of leadership—slow, but sure—matched his personality and appearance. A devout Roman Catholic, Rosecrans liked to gather his staff together for late-night religious discussions. In 1861, his victory at Rich Mountain, Virginia, made him one of the Union's earliest heroes. The following year he took command of the Army of the Cumberland.

MURFREESBORO: A COSTLY UNION VICTORY

On New Year's Day, 1863, Braxton Bragg telegraphed President Davis from Murfreesboro to announce a Confederate victory. Rosecrans's army, he said, "is falling back."

But the battle wasn't over yet. Rosecrans sent a Union force to occupy the high ground east of Stones River. On January 2, Bragg ordered John Breckinridge—a former U.S. vice president, now a Confederate general—to clear the Northerners from the hills. Breckinridge protested, fearing that his Kentuckians would be cut to pieces by Union artillery. But Bragg insisted. The attack began, and just as Breckinridge had predicted, his four brigades were badly hit. Breckinridge lost 1,500 men in less than an hour.

On January 3, Union reinforcements began to arrive. Bragg, sensing defeat after all, ordered a retreat to Tullahoma, Tennessee, twenty-five miles to the south. The Battle of Murfreesboro was a costly fight for both sides—12,000 dead, wounded, or captured for the Union, and slightly less for the Confederacy. Like the battles of Shiloh and Antietam, Murfreesboro was a Northern victory only in the sense that Union troops held the field when the fighting ended. Bragg still blocked the way into Chattanooga, the Union Army's goal in Tennessee.

Rosecrans's Northerners and Bragg's Confederates fight along Stones River in this Currier & Ives lithograph (right). After the battle wound down on New Year's Eve, a Louisiana private wrote, "The Earth was burdened with the Yankee dead. They were crossed and piled upon each other, nearly all of them lying on their backs, with their faces so ghastly turned up to the moon."

This wood-engraving (opposite, bottom), made from a sketch by a Union soldier, shows Northern reinforcements moving into battle as Bragg's Confederates try to break the Union line at "Hell's Half Acre," a grove of oak trees. "The enemy comes up directly," wrote John Beatty, commander of the 3rd Ohio Volunteer Infantry. "The roar of the guns to the right, left, and front of my brigade sounds like the continuous pounding of a thousand anvils."

A NEW KIND OF WAR

Of the roughly 82,000 men on both sides who fought at Murfreesboro, almost a fourth were killed, wounded, or captured in the battle. Casualty rates for many other Civil War battles were equal or worse.

The main reason for these heavy losses was that tactics did not keep pace with technology. Fighting methods had changed little since the days of Napoleon and George Washington. But innovations in weaponry made Civil War battlefields several times more deadly than those of the past.

In the 1700s and early 1800s, the chief infantry weapon was the Smoothbore musket, a firearm accurate up to only a few yards. Military manuals and training emphasized offensive tactics—bayonet charges and other sweeping movements in the open.

In the decades before the Civil War, however, improvements in the technology of firearms increased the range, accuracy, and firepower of infantry weapons, shifting the advantage from the offensive to the defensive. An infantryman in a protected position could fire about three shots per minute at an enemy 500 yards away. The offensive tactics of the past became suicidal.

However, few officers on either side realized that a revolution in military technology had taken place. They continued to do battle in the open, using outdated tactics, and as a result, thousands of men were killed and wounded at battles such as Antietam, Fredericksburg, and Murfreesboro.

The Civil War saw the first large-scale military use of railroads. The Union, with most of the country's industry and plenty of trained technicians, had a major advantage over the Confederacy when it came to using trains to move men and supplies. This photograph (right) shows the chief of the U.S. Military Railroads, General Herman Haupt (1817–1905; standing, upper right), checking the progress of a work crew. The locomotive of the work train is named after him.

Another technological advance that influenced military affairs was the telegraph. The Civil War was the first war in which military and political authorities far away from the fighting could be in instant communication with battlefield commanders. This communication gave presidents Lincoln and Davis a much greater degree of control over their generals than any previous wartime leaders. Timothy O'Sullivan took this photograph (opposite, bottom) of a Union telegraph crew encamped near Brandy Station, Virginia, preparing to string wires.

During the Civil War, the chief infantry weapon for both sides was the .58 caliber rifled musket (below), usually called the "Springfield," after the U.S. government armory at Springfield, Massachusetts, where they were manufactured. The Springfield used a new type of ammunition called the minié ball, which was not only more accurate and hard-hitting than earlier bullets, but could also be loaded more quickly.

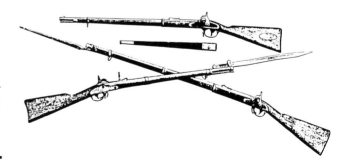

THE VICKSBURG CAMPAIGN

As 1862 drew to a close, General U. S. Grant's Army of the Tennessee had one goal—the capture of Confederate-held Vicksburg, Mississippi.

It was a daunting task. The city stood on a high bluff on the east bank of the Mississippi River, about halfway between Memphis and New Orleans. Confederate artillery batteries in and around Vicksburg commanded the river in all directions. The land to the west, on the Louisiana side of the river, was swampy, laced with lakes and countless bayous (small streams and rivers).

But Vicksburg had to be taken. The Confederacy controlled 400 miles of the Mississippi River—from Vicksburg to Port Hudson, Louisiana. This huge gap was the South's link with the West, and until it was closed, all the Union's earlier river victories, from Fort Henry to Memphis, would count for little.

The Union's Vicksburg Campaign began in November 1862. As winter set in, the Army of the Tennessee arrived in the swamps opposite Vicksburg, where the men built a camp they called Hard Times.

David Dixon Porter (1813–91; left) first went to sea at age ten, joined the Mexican Navy at fourteen, and finally entered the U.S. Navy two years later. Porter did so well in the Union Navy's capture of New Orleans that he was given command of the Union's Mississippi Squadron in late 1862. With the new job came a promotion to acting rear admiral, although there were more than eighty other officers ahead of Porter on the promotion list.

While General Sherman led his attack against Vicksburg by way of Chickasaw Bluffs, General John McClernand received approval from Washington to lead a second attack on the Mississippi River port. Yet instead of attacking Vicksburg as ordered, he moved his 29,000-man force up the Arkansas River (below) to Confederate-held Arkansas Post. With the support of thirteen gunboats under Admiral David Porter, Union troops forced a Confederate surrender. When the angry Grant learned of McClernand's operation, he ordered the Union troops back to Vicksburg.

WAR ON THE MISSISSIPPI

In the winter of 1863, Grant and William Tecumseh Sherman applied a new strategy in the campaign for the Mississippi River. Instead of attacking Vicksburg head-on, they decided to isolate it first. Vicksburg stood on a U-shaped bend in the river. Grant ordered his men to cut a canal across the bend, so that Union vessels could float downriver out of range of Confederate guns. Grant's men dug the canal, but the Mississippi River would not flow into it.

After several more fruitless attempts to bypass Vicksburg, Grant decided that the only way to capture the Confederate stronghold was to get his army across the river. Then they could attack the city overland from the east. The Union fleet, waiting north of Vicksburg, would have to make a dangerous passage right past the city.

On the night of April 16, 1863, several Union vessels slipped downriver. Sentries spotted them and lit bonfires, and Confederate gun crews quickly aimed and fired. All the vessels took hits, but only three small transports were sunk. The rest of the fleet made it downriver during the following week. On April 30, Grant's army began to cross the Mississippi, overwhelming a Confederate force at Port Gibson (south of Vicksburg). The overland campaign for Vicksburg had begun.

Commodore David Glasgow Farragut (1801–70; above) led the first Union effort to capture Vicksburg. Arriving outside the city with his fleet on May 18, 1862, Farragut ordered the city's military post to surrender. Confederate general Martin Luther Smith answered defiantly, "Mississippians don't know, and refuse to learn, how to surrender. If Commodore Farragut can teach them, let [him] come and try." Farragut's gunboats shelled the city, but steamed back to New Orleans when it became clear that Smith wasn't just boasting.

By 1863, Northern shipyards were turning out scores of ironclad gunboats for service on the Mississippi and other Western rivers. Shown here (opposite, top) is the Weehawken, a typical gunboat patterned after the Union's original ironclad, the Monitor. Life aboard an ironclad was usually cramped and uncomfortable for Northern sailors. When the boat was in action, the temperature below decks often went over 100 degrees, and the pounding of shells against iron plating sometimes deafened men permanently.

During the Vicksburg Campaign, Union forces fought many small amphibious operations in the swamps and bayous west of the Mississippi River. In this wood-engraving (right), Union troops prepare to attack a Confederate gunboat hidden along Louisiana's Bayou Teche. The gunboat, a converted three-decked river steamer, is draped with Spanish moss for camouflage.

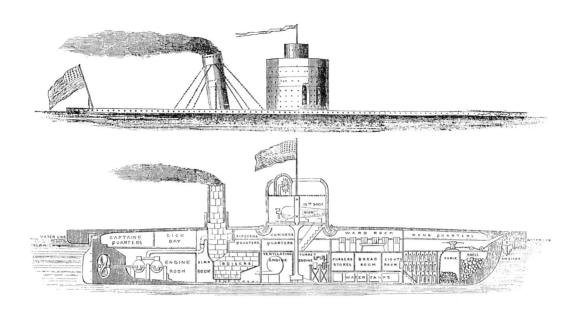

GRIERSON'S RAID

Throughout the Vicksburg Campaign, Confederate cavalry raiders harassed the rear of Grant's army. In December 1862, Nathan Bedford Forrest led 2,000 horsemen out of Tennessee to tear up railroad tracks, cut telegraph lines, and raid Union supply depots. Another raid by Earl Van Dorn captured Grant's base at Holly Springs, Mississippi. As a result, Grant had to cancel his plan to advance down the Mississippi Central Railroad toward Vicksburg.

In April 1863, as he prepared to cross the Mississippi, Grant ordered Colonel Benjamin Grierson to lead his 1,700-man cavalry brigade on a raid through Mississippi. Riding south from Tennessee, Grierson's cavalrymen swept down the length of the state, doing to the Confederacy what Forrest and Van Dorn had done to Grant. Grant hoped that Grierson would draw off Confederate troops from Vicksburg. When the Confederates pursued Grierson's cavalrymen, he tried to mislead them by sending small units off in different directions.

After riding over 600 miles in sixteen days, Grierson's troops reached the Union lines at Baton Rouge, Louisiana, with 500 prisoners captured along the way. The raid had achieved Grant's goal: The Confederates had sent a full infantry division after Grierson, along with most of the cavalry around Vicksburg, thus weakening the city's garrison.

Benjamin Grierson (1826–1911; above) was an unlikely candidate for fame as a cavalry commander. A music teacher from Illinois, he originally joined the infantry (foot soldiers) because he hated horses—one had kicked him in the head as a child, leaving a scar. Ironically, he found himself assigned to the cavalry in October 1861.

Mississippi militia tried to halt Grierson's raiders by burning bridges in their path. In this wood-engraving (opposite, top), the brigade's advance guard attacks a Southern unit as it starts to set fire to a bridge.

The Union horsemen's arrival in Baton Rouge, Louisiana, wasn't as dramatic as it appeared in this newspaper illustration (right). Many of Grierson's cavalrymen were so exhausted from their ordeal that they actually slept in the saddle as their footsore horses crossed Union lines. Grierson soon received a promotion to major general for what Lincoln called "his great raid through the heart of the Confederacy."

VICKSBURG: THE OVERLAND CAMPAIGN

At the beginning of May 1863, Grant's army numbered about 33,000 men. Jefferson Davis had ordered General John C. Pemberton, commander of the garrison at Vicksburg, to hold the city at all costs. Davis also ordered General Joseph E. Johnston to rush reinforcements to Mississippi to deal with Grant.

Grant's strategy was to capture Jackson, the capital of Mississippi and the hub of the state's road and railroad network, in order to keep reinforcements away from Pemberton. Then Grant would lure Pemberton out of Vicksburg's fortifications, beat him in battle, and take the city. In order to move fast and travel light, Grant ordered his men to carry only hard biscuits, salt, and coffee. Anything else they needed would come from the plantations along the way.

On May 14, Grant's army reached Jackson and quickly overran the city's 6,000 defenders. Johnston, convinced that Vicksburg was doomed, ordered Pemberton to join forces with him against Grant. Pemberton refused, but sent 20,000 men out of the city. On May 16, Grant attacked and defeated Pemberton's force at Champion's Hill, about halfway between Jackson and Memphis. Pemberton retreated to Vicksburg, leaving a force of 5,000 Confederates at Big Black River. Grant defeated them on May 17, driving the survivors back to Vicksburg. Within a week Grant's pursuing army arrived outside the city.

Although they served as commanders on opposing sides in the Battle of Jackson and throughout the war, Joseph Johnston (left) and William Sherman later became friends. Johnston died in 1891 after catching pneumonia at Sherman's funeral; despite cold, rainy weather at the ceremony, he refused to wear a hat, out of respect for his old adversary.

This lithograph (below) by Strobridge & Co. shows Union troops attacking a farm just outside Jackson, Mississippi. After capturing the area, General Sherman's troops destroyed its factories, warehouses, and railroad facilities. Fires soon spread to Jackson's houses. So many of them were destroyed that Union troops nicknamed the town "Chimneyville" because all that remained standing, in many places, were brick chimneys.

THE SIEGE OF VICKSBURG BEGINS

The Confederate defenses at Vicksburg were formidable. Soldiers manned a network of trenches and rifle pits surrounding the city, with plenty of artillery to back them up.

Encouraged by his army's successes at Jackson and Champion's Hill, Grant ordered a head-on assault for May 19, in spite of these strong defenses. The attack failed with heavy casualties, as the Confederates, firing from their well-protected trenches, cut down wave after wave of attacking bluecoats. "We did all that mortal men could do," reported a Union officer, "but such a slaughter!" Grant ordered another assault on May 22, which also failed. He realized that Vicksburg would have to be shelled and starved into surrender.

Grant's army dug trenches, moved in artillery, and began an almost nonstop bombardment of Vicksburg. Gunboats on the Mississippi echoed the Union Army's cannon fire. Inside the city, civilians abandoned their houses and dug shelters into the hillsides. Food ran low for soldiers and citizens alike. By June 28, Pemberton's men were down to one biscuit and a scrap of bacon per day, while the townspeople lived on rats and mule meat. By July, it was clear that Vicksburg couldn't hold out much longer.

John Clifford Pemberton (1814–81; left) was a native of Philadelphia, but after Fort Sumter his friendship with Southern officers—and the fact that his wife was a Virginian—led him to resign his U.S. Army commission and join the Confederacy. Two of his brothers fought in the Union Army.

In order to cross the Mississippi River and attack Vicksburg from the rear, Grant's army began to dig the Vicksburg Neck Canal (below). Grant hoped that the river would change its course and flow through the canal, isolating Vicksburg and opening up a strip of land south of the city where the Union troops could cross. The plan, however, completely failed when spring floods washed out the canal.

THE UNION ATTACKS CHARLESTON

In the spring of 1863, while Grant was planning his assault on Vicksburg, the Union high command decided to launch a campaign against Charleston, South Carolina. The capture of this major Southern port would help tighten the blockade, and boost morale in the North. Secession had started in Charleston, and the war had begun with the Confederate attack on Fort Sumter in the city's harbor.

Charleston was heavily defended by two island forts, Fort Sumter and Fort Moultrie. They blocked the harbor entrance, and there were many fortifications inside. An English observer wrote, "both sides of the harbor for several miles appear to bristle with heavy guns."

Navy Secretary Gideon Welles believed that the Navy could take the city by battering down the two island forts. He gave the assignment to Rear Admiral Samuel Du Pont, commander of the South Atlantic Blockading Squadron. On April 7, nine ironclads steamed into Charleston harbor.

The harbor erupted in smoke and flames as the forts' guns fired on the Union fleet. They threw so many shells that the ironclads barely managed to return fire. At sundown, after hours of bombardment from the Confederate batteries, the ironclads withdrew. Only one was sunk, but five were completely disabled. It was the Union Navy's worst setback of the war. Welles and Du Pont blamed each other for the failure, and Du Pont soon resigned.

George S. Cook photographed the gunners of the Confederacy's "Palmetto Battery" (right) standing ready to defend Charleston from the Union's naval attack. (The palmetto plant was the symbol of South Carolina.) The general in charge of Charleston's defenses was P.G.T. Beauregard, who had also commanded the Confederate siege of Fort Sumter two years before.

This dramatic Currier & Ives lithograph (below) depicts the furious fire from the Confederate forts protecting Charleston Harbor. In the first forty minutes of the battle, Southern guns fired over 2,000 shells at Du Pont's Union fleet, severely damaging five of the nine leading ships. Captain John Rodgers, commander of the Union ironclad Weehawken, *later wrote, "I was surprised to find that these vessels could be so much injured in so short a time."*

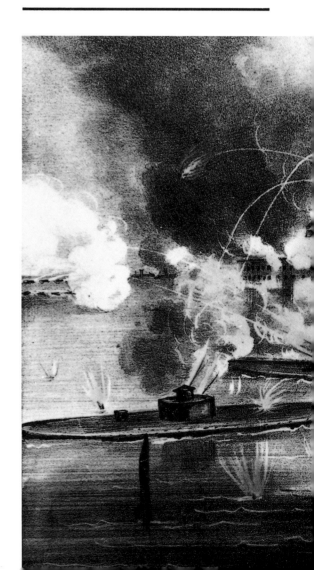

FORT WAGNER

The Union Navy tried again in July. This time, the expedition's leader was Rear Admiral John Dahlgren, with 15,000 soldiers accompanying the fleet. Dahlgren planned to land the troops on Morris Island and use the island as a base for bombarding Fort Sumter.

Among the troops was the 54th Massachusetts Regiment, a unit of black soldiers. Their commander was Colonel Robert Gould Shaw, a young white Bostonian from an abolitionist family. The Union government had only recently approved recruitment of black troops, and Shaw intended to prove that black troops would fight for freedom as bravely as white soldiers.

The 54th and the rest of the Union landing force reached Morris Island safely, but the Confederates still held two strong positions, Fort Gregg and Fort Wagner. On July 18, the 54th led an assault on Fort Wagner. The regiment charged into a storm of artillery and rifle fire. Half its men fell dead (Shaw among them) or wounded, but the survivors reached the fort and overtook part of it before darkness and heavy fire forced them back.

Despite the setback, the 54th's gallant action showed the North that black soldiers would fight and fight well. The influential *Atlantic Monthly* stated, "Through the cannon smoke of that dark night, the manhood of the colored race shines before many eyes that would not see."

In this dramatic lithograph by Kurz and Allison, the 54th Massachusetts regiment reaches the edge of Fort Wagner, yards from Confederate fire. Sergeant William Carney, who grabbed the regiment's flag as the flag bearer fell dead, became the first of sixteen black Civil War soldiers to win the Medal of Honor. (He had to wait over twenty years, however, for Congress to make the award official.) Among those killed was Colonel Shaw of the 54th; the Confederates buried him in a common grave with his troops. After the war, Union authorities located the grave and offered to send Shaw's body back to Boston for burial. His parents turned down the offer, saying "We can imagine no holier place than where he is."

THE UNION ARMY RETURNS TO VIRGINIA

On January 20, 1863, the Army of the Potomac marched out on yet another advance against Richmond. This time, the offensive was halted not by Robert E. Lee, but by weather. Cold rains turned the country roads of Virginia into rivers of mud, making movement impossible.

After this miserable "mud march," President Lincoln relieved Ambrose Burnside of command, replacing him with General Joseph Hooker. Hooker had done well in the Peninsular Campaign, where he won the nickname "Fighting Joe." Throughout the winter, Hooker did an admirable job of organizing, training, and raising the spirits of the discouraged troops. As spring began, the general brimmed with confidence. The question, he told Lincoln, was not if he would take Richmond, but when.

Hooker planned to deceive Lee by leaving a small Union force at Fredericksburg. The rest of his army would cross the Rappahannock and Rapidan rivers upstream from the town. Lee, Hooker hoped, would be forced to fight in the open, where the Union's superior numbers would prevail.

On April 27, the Army of the Potomac began moving. On April 30, Hooker's main force reached a crossroads town called Chancellorsville, less than ten miles from the Army of Northern Virginia's base at Fredericksburg.

Joseph Hooker (1814–79; left) was a rancher in California when war broke out. He had to borrow $700 from a San Francisco restaurant owner to travel east to offer his services to the Union. Some Northern politicians criticized Lincoln for giving Hooker command of the Army of the Potomac because Hooker had once remarked that the Union needed a dictator to wage war successfully against the Confederacy.

On May 1, Robert E. Lee and Stonewall Jackson met about a mile southeast of Chancellorsville to make plans for the upcoming battle. At eight o'clock the next morning, the two generals saddled up and prepared to move their troops into position. Stonewall Jackson pointed to the west, where he was to attack; Lee nodded, and Jackson rode off. It was the last time they saw each other. This lithograph (below), from a painting by J. G. Fay, portrays the final meeting of the two great commanders.

CHANCELLORSVILLE

Before the war, Joseph Hooker and cavalryman George Stoneman often played poker. "He could play the best game of poker I ever saw," Stoneman said, "until it came to the point where he should go a thousand better, and then he would flunk [fold]."

At Chancellorsville, Joseph Hooker "flunked." For reasons still unclear, he ordered a halt. Despite a brilliant battle plan, the general's nerve failed when the time came to carry it out. The next move was up to Robert E. Lee, perhaps the greatest gambler of them all.

Lee realized that the small Union force outside of Fredericksburg posed no real threat. Leaving 10,000 men at Fredericksburg, he marched north to take on Hooker. Then Lee raised the stakes. In a daring move, he divided his already outnumbered army by sending 23,000 men under Stonewall Jackson to attack Hooker's right flank.

As the sun began to set on May 2, the soldiers of the Union's XI Corps were resting outside a thick forest called the Wilderness. Suddenly deer, rabbits, and even a bear ran out of the woods in terror. Then Jackson's infantry burst through the trees, screaming the high-pitched "Rebel yell." The Northerners fled. By nightfall, the Confederates had pushed Union forces back across a broad front. Skirmishing continued in the moonlight. One of the casualties was Stonewall Jackson, shot in the arm by a Confederate soldier who mistook him for a Union cavalryman.

Stonewall Jackson (1824–63; left) had to move his 31,000 troops carefully; they were marching directly in front of the Army of the Potomac's right flank. If they were discovered, Hooker might overwhelm Jackson's outnumbered men and put Lee and his troops in danger. Because of the need for caution, it was late in the afternoon before Jackson's infantry finally reached the jump-off point for their attack.

While his troops sweep the men of the Union's XI Corps from the battlefield, Confederate bullets strike Stonewall Jackson in this Kurz & Allison lithograph. "My own men," Jackson muttered as his officers helped him from his panicked horse. With two bullets in his left arm, Jackson endured an agonizing two hours until stretcher bearers brought him to a field hospital set up in a local tavern.

CONFEDERATE TRIUMPH AND TRAGEDY

During the morning of May 3, Hooker's commanders fought fiercely around Chancellorsville to keep the Army of the Potomac from collapsing under repeated Southern assaults. Fighting continued the next day. By then the Union forces had pulled together and established a strong defensive position. Some officers, knowing that Lee was still greatly outnumbered, urged Hooker to launch a counterattack. But, on the night of May 5, Hooker ordered a retreat instead. By the end of the next day, his army was safely across the Rappahannock River. Union casualties for the three-day battle were 17,000; the Army of Northern Virginia lost about 13,000 men.

Chancellorsville was a triumph of generalship and perhaps the South's greatest victory. In the North, shock and dismay followed word of the Union's latest defeat. Lincoln was shocked by the news. He paced the floor of Washington's telegraph office, saying, "My God! My God! What will the country say?"

But a tragedy tarnished the Confederacy's success: the loss of Stonewall Jackson. His left arm was amputated on May 2, but doctors felt confident that he would recover. Then, on May 7, pneumonia set in. "God will not take him from us now that we need him so much," said Lee. On May 10, however, the great Stonewall died.

Using stretchers improvised from rifles and blankets, Union troops rescue wounded comrades (left) as the dense undergrowth of the Wilderness catches fire. Poet Walt Whitman, who witnessed this scene while searching for his brother, a wounded Union soldier, recorded his impressions in his journal: "—and still the woods on fire—still many are not only skorch'd—too many, unable to move, are burn'd to death . . . "

On May 3, Union general John Sedgwick attacked Confederate positions at Fredericksburg, in a battle sometimes called "Second Chancellorsville." Lee quickly moved troops to block Sedgwick's advance, preventing him from aiding Hooker at Chancellorsville. Captain A. J. Russell took this photograph (below) of Confederate dead lying along the stone wall in front of Marye's Heights at Fredericksburg.

THE BATTLE OF BRANDY STATION

Cavalry played a minor role in most Civil War battles. Advances in firearms and artillery made the large-scale cavalry charges of the past too dangerous. Instead, both sides used cavalry for reconnaissance, for protecting the flanks of marching armies, and for raiding the supply lines of the opposition.

At the start of the war, the Confederate cavalry was superior to the Union's, mostly because Southerners were more at home on horseback than city-bred Northerners. The Confederacy also had several excellent cavalry commanders, including J.E.B. Stuart in the East, and Nathan Bedford Forrest, who led spectacular raids deep behind Union lines in the West.

By 1863, however, the Union cavalry had become a better match for the Confederates. In the Vicksburg Campaign, Colonel Benjamin Grierson proved that Northern horsemen could raid behind enemy lines, too. In the East, General Alfred Pleasonton organized the Army of the Potomac's cavalry into a formidable fighting force.

In June, General Joseph Hooker sent Pleasonton and 10,000 troopers into Culpeper County, Virginia, to determine the position of Lee's army. On June 9, the Union cavalrymen ran into J.E.B. Stuart's 8,000 horsemen at Brandy Station, and the biggest cavalry fight of the war was on. The two sides fought at close range with sabers and pistols until Confederate infantry arrived. Pleasonton was forced to withdraw, but he had confirmed Hooker's suspicion that Lee was preparing his army for a major campaign.

On June 9, Union general Pleasonton surprised the Army of Northern Virginia's cavalry commander J.E.B. Stuart (right), and fought to a draw one of the war's few cavalry battles. Embarrassed and worried about his reputation, Stuart sought revenge by raiding behind Union lines during the Confederacy's upcoming invasion of the North—instead of reporting the Army of the Potomac's activities to Robert E. Lee.

By the end of 1863, Brandy Station was a major base for the Army of the Potomac. This photograph (below) shows men of a Union Zouave regiment at their camp at Brandy Station. (Zouaves wore colorful uniforms based on those used by French troops in North Africa.)

LEE MOVES NORTH

At the beginning of the summer of 1863, Robert E. Lee convinced Jefferson Davis that the time had come for a massive strike at the Union's heartland. Despite his army's victories at Fredericksburg and Chancellorsville, Lee saw clearly that the Union's strength and manpower could only increase. The time to invade was now, Lee argued, while the Army of Northern Virginia was at the height of its power and confidence.

Lee made a good case for his plan. First, he told Davis, a thrust into the North might force Lincoln to order Grant and his army east, easing the pressure on Vicksburg. Second, a Union defeat on Northern soil would further dishearten the Union public, who might then call more strongly for a negotiated peace. Third, a successful foray might finally convince Britain and France to intervene on the side of the South. And Lee, ever the gambler, cherished the hope that he might destroy the Union Army and force Lincoln to ask for peace.

On June 3, the first elements of Lee's army left Fredericksburg and moved north. His plan was to advance through the Blue Ridge Mountains, cross the Potomac River into Maryland, and march into Pennsylvania. Once in Pennsylvania, Lee hoped to capture the state capital, Harrisburg, and move toward Philadelphia. The main body of the Army of Northern Virginia, about 70,000 men, crossed into Maryland on June 16. By the end of June, the Confederates were across the Pennsylvania line.

"We should not conceal from ourselves," wrote Robert E. Lee to Jefferson Davis, "that our resources in men are constantly diminishing . . . " Lee (on horseback, above) knew that his army would face dangerous odds in its second invasion of the North, but he had confidence in his men. "General Lee believed that the Army of Northern Virginia . . . could accomplish anything," one of his officers later wrote.

President Lincoln replaced Joseph Hooker with George Gordon Meade (1815–72) on June 27, 1863. Meade, the bearded man standing at the center of this photograph (opposite, top), had a reputation as a competent, methodical, but short-tempered soldier. Like Ambrose Burnside before him, he at first refused command of the Army of the Potomac. When he learned that Lincoln had personally selected him for the post, Meade replied, "Well, I've been tried and condemned without a hearing, and I suppose I shall have to go to the execution."

This wood-engraving (opposite, bottom) shows the Army of Northern Virginia crossing the Potomac River at Williamsport, Maryland. "Well, boys, I've been seceding for two years, and now I've got back into the Union again!" shouted one Southern soldier as he waded ashore on the Maryland side.

Part II
Triumph and Turmoil for the Union

The capture of Vicksburg by General Ulysses S. Grant on July 4, 1863, ended six weeks of siege and more than eight months of campaigning on land and water by Union forces. In the North, news of the city's capture, coming just after the Union victory at Gettysburg, "excited a degree of enthusiasm not excelled during the war," wrote Secretary of the Navy Gideon Welles.

For three days the Army of the Potomac and the Army of Northern Virginia clashed at Gettysburg, Pennsylvania, in the largest single engagement of the Civil War. When it was over—on July 4, 1863—Lee's beaten army began a retreat back to Virginia.

On the same day, Vicksburg surrendered to Ulysses S. Grant, ending a long siege. The Union now had control of the Mississippi River, the South's lifeline to the West. The loss of Vicksburg probably contributed more to the Confederacy's downfall than its defeat at Gettysburg.

Together, the Union's twin victories at Gettysburg and Vicksburg marked the turning point of the Civil War. The Confederacy would still win battlefield victories, but from now on the South would be fighting not just for its independence but for its survival.

As the second half of the year began, the focus of the Union war effort shifted to Tennessee. Union forces had suffered a bloody defeat at Chickamauga and retreated into Chattanooga, where the Confederates held them under siege. Then Grant arrived on the scene. In November, he swept the Confederates away from Chattanooga at Lookout Mountain and Missionary Ridge.

Thus the South's hopes were raised and then dashed. Davis, addressing a downcast Confederate Congress, admitted, "We now know that the only reliable hope for peace is the vigor of our resistance." While in Washington, Abraham Lincoln felt confident enough to outline plans for the South's "reconstruction" after the war.

GETTYSBURG: THE BATTLEFIELD

Lee's soldiers advanced through the Pennsylvania countryside. The Southerners treated the region's white civilians reasonably well, but when they found free blacks they sent them south to be sold into slavery.

By this time, the 90,000 soldiers of the Army of the Potomac were marching north from Frederick, Maryland, in pursuit. General George Meade, Joseph Hooker's replacement as commander of the Army of the Potomac, moved as fast as he dared, but he had to keep his army between Lee and Washington. Lee, too, had to move with caution, since he didn't know where the Union Army was. J.E.B. Stuart was under orders to keep in close contact and report Meade's movements, but the flamboyant horseman and his cavalry rode off on a pointless raid against Meade's supply lines instead.

Lee was also wary of making a rash move against Meade. He had hoped to fight Joseph Hooker, who had panicked so easily at Chancellorsville. Meade, in Lee's judgment, was a different sort of general. "General Meade will make no mistake in my front," he told his staff, "and if I make one, he will make haste to take advantage of it."

The Army of the Potomac and the Army of Northern Virginia converged near two towns, Gettysburg and Cashtown. On June 30, Union cavalry skirmished with Confederate soldiers outside Gettysburg. Thinking that Gettysburg was Lee's objective, Meade decided to move his army there.

Four ridges surrounded Gettysburg, and the need to seize and hold these pieces of high ground played a major role in the battle. For most of the conflict, Union forces held a defensive line shaped like a fishhook. The tip of the fishhook was Culp's Hill (lower left in the drawing) with its shank curving southwest along Cemetery Hill and Cemetery Ridge. It ended at Big and Little Round Top (lower right). The main Confederate line ran along Seminary Ridge to the west of the town. Although several major roads passed through Gettysburg, its importance as a road junction wasn't a major consideration for the Union and Confederate commanders.

THE FIRST CLASH

What made Gettysburg the site of the greatest battle of the Civil War (and the biggest battle ever fought in the Western Hemisphere) was a rumor that the town held a supply of shoes.

Confederate general Henry Heth's division had marched into Pennsylvania on bare feet. On the night of June 30, he asked Commander A. P. Hill for permission to send his men into Gettysburg to look for shoes. Hill agreed, asking Heth to determine Union troop strength on the Chambersburg Pike, the road leading into Gettysburg from the north.

Early on the morning of July 1, Heth's division moved down the road toward Gettysburg. Suddenly gunfire crackled in the morning air. Union troops—cavalrymen of General John Buford's brigade—blocked the road.

Buford's men were outnumbered two to one and lacked artillery, but they kept up heavy fire on the advancing Confederates. Eventually, Buford ordered his troops to fall back to the high ground of McPherson's Ridge. At 10:00 a.m., General John Reynolds, commander of the Union's I Corps, arrived on the ridge to confer with Buford. (A corps was a unit of two or more divisions; each Confederate corps at Gettysburg numbered about 22,000 men, Union corps about 11,000). Reynolds ordered Buford to hold his ground, then sent a note to Meade urging him to march faster to Gettysburg. Next, Reynolds ordered General Oliver O. Howard to bring up his corps to help Buford keep the Confederates out of the town. By 11:00 a.m., the Battle of Gettysburg had begun in earnest.

A. P. (Ambrose Powell) Hill of Virginia (1825–65; above) fought under—and with—Stonewall Jackson until the Battle of Chancellorsville. The two headstrong generals didn't get along, and Jackson actually put Hill under arrest just before the Battle of Antietam. At Gettysburg, Hill commanded the Army of Northern Virginian's II Corps.

Mathew Brady took this photograph of Kentucky-born cavalry general John Buford (1826–63; seated) and his staff. "He is of a good-natured disposition," a friend said of him, "but not to be trifled with." At Gettysburg, Buford's Union cavalrymen fought with the new seven-shot Spencer repeating rifle. Southern soldiers called the weapon "The Yankee gun that can load on Sunday and shoot all week."

FROM SKIRMISH TO BATTLE

Shortly after sending his message to Meade, Reynolds rode forward to rally the troops facing Heth's Confederates. A sniper shot him off his horse, and General Reynolds, considered one of the Army of the Potomac's best officers, died.

The outnumbered Union troops began to fall back as A. P. Hill fed in more Southern troops. Meanwhile, a Confederate corps led by Richard Ewell started moving into Gettysburg from the north.

Facing Ewell were the soldiers of the Union's XI Corps, commanded by General Howard. The men of the XI Corps resisted the Confederate advance at first, until Ewell sent Major General Jubal Early's division into the fight. Howard's soldiers fell back, retreating through Gettysburg, and 4,000 men were taken prisoner.

Lee arrived outside Gettysburg in mid-afternoon. Still unsure of the strength of the Union force, he ordered Hill and Ewell to hold back. But Lee quickly realized that the collapse of the XI Corps left the troops facing A. P. Hill without support. At 4:00 p.m., the attacks resumed. Both Union lines gave way, and soon the Southerners captured the town of Gettysburg itself.

One hope remained for the Union. One of Howard's divisions still held Cemetery Hill, just to the south of Gettysburg. The survivors of the day's fighting rushed to the safety of this precious piece of high ground.

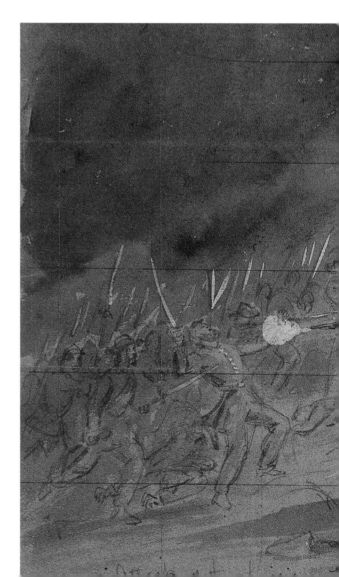

Richard Stoddard Ewell (1817–72; left) commanded what was formerly Stonewall Jackson's III Corps. He was severely wounded at the Second Battle of Bull Run, but returned to duty in May 1863 with a wooden leg. Called "Old Bald Head" by his men, Ewell was angry with Lee during the first day's fighting. He was preparing to capture Harrisburg, Pennsylvania's capital, when the order came to shift his troops to meet the Union troops at Gettysburg.

In this drawing (below) by A. R. Waud, the Confederacy's "Louisiana Tigers" sweep down on an artillery battery of the Union's XI Corps as a gun crew tries to push its cannons to safety. The men of the XI, many of them German immigrants, went into battle eager to avenge their humiliation at Chancellorsville, but they soon found themselves in retreat once again.

THE FIRST DAY'S FIGHTING ENDS

Meade quickly grasped the importance of the morning's events at Gettysburg. "Good God!" he said when he received Reynolds's message, "if the enemy gets Gettysburg we are lost." Learning that Reynolds had fallen, Meade sent one of his best generals, Winfield Scott Hancock, to oversee the fighting.

Although the Union troops held a strong position, one good push might have driven them off the high ground. But Lee, still without Stuart's cavalry to provide intelligence, didn't know just how weak the Northern forces were. He instructed Ewell to assault Cemetery Hill "if possible." Ewell, lacking the aggressive instinct of his former commander, Stonewall Jackson, decided it wasn't possible. As night fell, reinforcements began to reach the Union line.

Still, Lee felt confident on the night of July 1, and told his generals, "we will attack the enemy in the morning as early as practicable." His battle plan called for coordinated attacks along Meade's lines. General James Longstreet, commander of the Confederate Army's I Corps, strongly objected to Lee's strategy. Longstreet wanted to break off the fight at Gettysburg and move between the Army of the Potomac and Washington. With the Union capital threatened, Meade reasoned that he would have to attack Lee, rather than the other way around. Lee vetoed the idea. "The enemy is there," said Lee, "and I am going to whip him there, or he is going to whip me."

Many regarded Winfield Scott Hancock (1824–86; above), a hero of the Battle of Chancellorsville, as the Army of the Potomac's best fighting general. His efforts on the first day of fighting at Gettysburg kept a bad situation from turning into disaster. "His mere presence was a reinforcement, and everybody on the field felt stronger for his being there," wrote Union general Carl Schurz. When a fellow officer suggested that he withdraw his outnumbered troops from Cemetery Hill, Hancock replied, "Sir! I am in command on this field. Send every man you have got!"

The 24th Michigan Infantry, part of the Army of the Potomac's famed "Iron Brigade," lost 399 of its 496 soldiers by the end of the first day's fighting at Gettysburg. Although they were volunteers, the men of the unit wore the short black hat of the Regular Army as a mark of distinction. The men of Lee's army called them "those damned black hats." Timothy O'Sullivan photographed several of the 24th's dead on the battlefield (right).

THE DEVIL'S DEN AND THE PEACH ORCHARD

Meade arrived at Cemetery Hill early on the morning of July 2. Lee already had his entire army in position, while much of the Army of the Potomac was still marching to the battlefield. Instead of attacking Lee, Meade decided to strengthen the Union's high-ground defensive line.

Although Lee had planned for early action, it was mid-afternoon before Longstreet's 15,000 troops were in position for their attack on Meade's left. Lee wanted to strike the Union forces through a peach orchard in front of Cemetery Ridge, but scouts found it occupied by Union soldiers.

The troops belonged to General Dan Sickles's III Corps. Acting without orders, Sickles had moved his men a half-mile forward of the main Union line, opening a gap in Meade's defensive line. Although this unexpected obstacle foiled Lee's original plan, Longstreet ordered a division to attack Sickles's men through a boulder-strewn field called the Devil's Den. At 4:00 p.m. the attack began. Union and Confederate troops tangled in close-range combat among the rocks. Despite fierce resistance, Longstreet's men slowly pushed the Northerners back. Sickles himself was carried off the field with a shattered leg. (His wound probably saved him from a court-martial.) Fighting in and around the peach orchard continued for the rest of the day, but now the focus of the battle shifted to the Round Tops, two hills at the southern end of Cemetery Ridge.

Confederate troops prepare to skirmish in a wheat field adjoining the Union-held peach orchard in this painting by Edwin Forbes. "A burst of cheering, followed by a violent musketry fire, told us the rebels were charging," wrote a Union officer who took part in the clash. "It was a hard fight. The Confederates appeared to have the devil in them . . . men fell dead and wounded with frightful rapidity."

THE FIGHT FOR LITTLE ROUND TOP

The smaller of the two hills, Little Round Top, was the southern anchor of Meade's entire defensive line. If Lee's troops seized the hill and moved artillery to its summit, the Union would have to abandon Cemetery Ridge and almost certainly lose the battle. Sickles's unauthorized move had left this important piece of ground undefended on the afternoon of July 2.

General Gouverneur Warren, a signal officer acting as Meade's chief of staff, realized the danger at Little Round Top. He caught site of an Alabama brigade preparing to charge up the hill and quickly ordered a passing Union brigade into action. The Yankees hauled a cannon up the slopes and reached the summit just as the Confederate assault began.

The 20th Maine Volunteers bore the brunt of the attack. Their leader, Colonel Joshua Chamberlain, a former college professor, realized that the outcome of the battle—and perhaps even the war—depended on his leadership and the courage of his men.

The Alabama brigade drove the Maine men from their positions five times, but the Northerners recaptured their ground each time. Finally, when their ammunition had run out, Chamberlain ordered his men to fix bayonets and charge the Confederates. The shocked Southerners fell back—and ran into another company of Union troops hiding behind a stone wall. The Confederates fled. Little Round Top remained in Union hands.

The men of Colonel William Oates's 15th Alabama brigade prepare to assault Little Round Top in this painting (above) by Edwin Forbes. At this point in the battle, only a small detachment of Union signalmen occupied the crucial hill. The glint of the Confederate regiment's bayonets in the July sun alerted General Warren to the danger at Little Round Top.

The dead of the 15th Alabama and the 20th Maine brigades lie together in the "slaughter pen" at Little Round Top. The fierce fighting at close quarters produced terrible casualties; half of Colonel Chamberlain's men fell during the fight, and a Texas brigade that joined in the battle had all but one of its officers killed or wounded. "The blood stood in puddles in some places among the rocks," wrote Colonel Oates.

CEMETERY HILL AND CULP'S HILL

While savage fighting continued around the Round Tops, another part of Longstreet's Corps went into action a mile to the north. Here, Lee's objective was the center of the Union line along Cemetery Ridge.

As at Little Round Top, an Alabama regiment was the spearhead of the Confederate assault. There was also a gap in the Union line, which General Winfield Scott Hancock tried to fill by rushing in troops. Meanwhile, only one Union regiment, the 1st Minnesota, stood between the Confederates and their goal. Hancock ordered the 260 men of the 1st Minnesota to charge the 1,600 Confederates, in order to buy time for the arrival of the reinforcements. The Minnesota regiment did its job, but only forty-seven men survived their gallant charge unscathed. A Georgia brigade managed to reach the summit, but was driven back.

As the shadows lengthened, Richard Ewell's men went forward to seize Culp's Hill, just to the west of Cemetery Hill. The hill was thinly defended: Most of the Union troops in the area had been moved to other parts of the battlefield. A Confederate force led by General "Allegheny Ed" Johnson managed to capture some Union trenches at the hill's base, but a Union brigade arrived after sundown and drove them off. Two more Confederate brigades attacked Cemetery Hill and they too were beaten back as night settled on the battlefield.

Cemetery Hill's Union defenders rally as Early's Confederates charge toward the cemetery gate in this painting by Edwin Forbes (right). Some Northern soldiers noticed, with bitter amusement, a sign on the gate warning that anyone using firearms on the cemetery grounds would be arrested.

The assault on July 2 marked the farthest penetration into Union lines. Winfield Scott Hancock, however, realized the danger and rushed reinforcements to the hill, denying the Southerners a chance to break through Meade's defenses. This eyewitness sketch by A. R. Waud (opposite, bottom) shows a Union artillery battery on Cemetery Hill going into action as Jubal Early's Confederates launch their twilight attack.

This map (below) shows the position of Lee's and Meade's forces at the end of the fighting on July 2. The Union positions curled southwest from Culp's Hill to the Round Tops—the famous "fishhook." The Confederate II Corps, commanded by Richard Ewell, was north of Culp's and Cemetery hills as the day ended; A. P. Hill's III Corps held a line extending south of Seminary Ridge, roughly parallel to the Union-held Cemetery Ridge; and James Longstreet's I Corps was in position along the Emmitsburg Road leading into Gettysburg from the south.

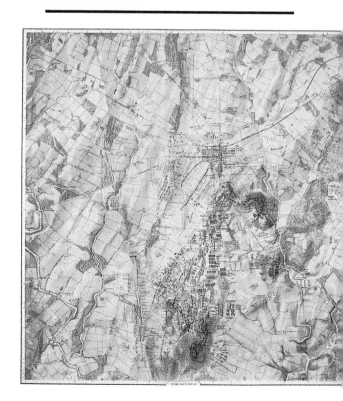

Entrenched guns
Stevens Battery
Gettysburg or left
Louisiana Tigers

THE THIRD MORNING

The second day of fighting at Gettysburg ended with few gains for the Confederacy. Lee's well-coordinated assaults had failed and Meade still held a strong line stretching from the Round Tops to Culp's Hill.

Despite the loss of 7,000 men on July 1 and 9,000 on July 2, Lee remained confident. He sketched out plans for a three-pronged attack on July 3. Beginning with a massive artillery bombardment, three infantry divisions would charge straight at Cemetery Ridge. Then J.E.B. Stuart (who had finally arrived early on the morning of July 2) would come at Meade from the rear while Ewell attacked the Union right.

The Union generals met at midnight at Meade's headquarters. Meade's plan was simple: Hold fast and meet the attack Lee was bound to make.

July 3 began with a Union attack on the remaining Confederate troops on Culp's Hill. Apart from this, there was little fighting. Then, just after 1:00 p.m., the Confederate bombardment began. More than 150 cannons pounded the Union defenses.

Two hours later, Longstreet ordered the infantry to move forward from Seminary Ridge, the Confederate front line. The 4,000 Virginians of George Pickett's division spearheaded the assault, which came to be known as Pickett's Charge.

In this illustration (right), a mournful James Longstreet orders George Pickett (on horseback) and his men forward on the afternoon of July 3. (Pickett, however, did not actually charge with his men.) As he had on July 1, Longstreet opposed Lee's battle plan. "General," he said after learning that Lee desired a frontal assault on Meade's lines, "I have been a soldier all of my life . . . and [I] know as well as anyone what soldiers can do. It is my opinion that no 15,000 men ever arrayed for battle can take that position."

Only about 6,000 Yankees held the center of the Union line along Cemetery Ridge where Lee planned to strike hardest, but they were well dug in with plenty of artillery support. Some of these soldiers reported that a strange silence, "as still as the sabbath day," settled over the Union defenses just before Longstreet's artillery began its bombardment. This drawing (below) shows the Union encampment.

PICKETT'S CHARGE

At 3:00 p.m., under a blazing July sun, 15,000 Confederate infantrymen marched into the valley between Seminary and Cemetery ridges. The mile-wide line swept forward at a walking pace.

Then the Union guns opened up. As the first shells hit, huge gaps opened up in the Confederate line, but other men stepped up to take the places of those who fell.

Next, the Confederates came in range of the Union infantrymen's rifles. A sheet of flame lit up Cemetery Ridge. Still the Confederates marched, yelling now, even though whole regiments disappeared under the fire of Meade's men. One Confederate unit fixed bayonets and charged an angle of the stone wall running along Cemetery Ridge. Its commander, General Lewis Armistead, died with his hand on the muzzle of a Union cannon.

The Confederates fell back in the face of the Union's massed firepower. A half hour after it had begun, Pickett's Charge was over. Less than half of the Confederates who had begun the attack came back to Seminary Ridge.

Lee mounted his horse, Traveller, and went out to meet the survivors as they staggered in. "It's all my fault," he said, fighting back tears, "it's all my fault."

This lithograph portrays the high point of Pickett's Charge: the Confederate assault on the angle of the stone wall along Cemetery Ridge. Winfield Scott Hancock, in the thick of the fighting, went down when a Southern bullet hit his saddle and drove a nail into his leg. A short distance away, Confederate general Lewis Armistead, a pre-war friend of Hancock's, lay dying after his valiant charge at the Union guns. With his last breath, Armistead asked Hancock to take his watch and spurs and return them to his family.

THE UNION VICTORIOUS

The failure of Pickett's Charge ended Lee's hopes for a decisive victory at Gettysburg. Anticipating a Union counterattack, Lee ordered his remaining men to reform their lines. Coming across George Pickett, Lee told the downcast Virginian to move his division into position. Pickett replied, "General Lee, I have no division now."

Meade decided against renewing the fight, although several of his generals urged him to do so. He had no desire to risk his army's gains by attacking Lee, who had proved his skill as a defensive fighter many times. "We have done well enough," he said. For the first time, the Army of the Potomac had won a clear victory over the Army of Northern Virginia.

July 4, 1863, marked the eighty-seventh anniversary of the independence of the United States, a nation now divided, from Britain. All morning, Lee waited for the Union counterattack. At 1:00 p.m., a few Union brigades moved down from Cemetery Ridge. Then it began to rain, and the Union troops halted. The Battle of Gettysburg was over.

Lee now turned to the task of getting his army safely back to Virginia. The wounded were already on their way, in a wagon convoy seventeen miles long. That night, the rest of the Army of Northern Virginia followed. It was several days before Meade and the weary Union Army moved out of Gettysburg to pursue the retreating Confederates.

In a driving rain, the Army of the Potomac marches out of Gettysburg and begins its slow pursuit of the retreating Army of Northern Virginia. "Too many of our officers think it sufficient if the Rebels quit and go off," wrote Navy Secretary Gideon Welles when he learned that Meade had waited until July 7 to get his troops on the road. Meade may have acted with caution because his three most aggressive corps commanders—John Reynolds, Dan Sickles, and Winfield Scott Hancock—had all been killed or wounded at Gettysburg.

GETTYSBURG: THE AFTERMATH

The news from Gettysburg sent a wave of joy and relief through the North. A Northern official wrote, "The results of this victory are priceless. Philadelphia, Washington, and Baltimore are safe. The rebels are hunted out of the North, their best army is routed, and the charm of Lee's invincibility broken."

But Lincoln's joy at the Union victories soon turned to anger at Meade. He had expected the Union commander to catch and destroy Lee's army. But Meade continued to move slowly, despite repeated telegrams from the president and from General in Chief Henry Halleck urging him forward. Meade replied that his army was exhausted and that rain had turned the Pennsylvania roads to mud.

The same rains that slowed Meade had swelled the Potomac River, which Lee needed to cross to reach safety. On July 7, Lee's army began arriving at Williamsport, Maryland, where he intended to cross. Confederate engineers worked frantically to build a pontoon bridge across the Potomac. Meade reached Williamsport on July 12, but waited until the 14th to attack. When he did, he found the Confederate positions empty. Lee's army had crossed on the night of July 13, leaving campfires burning to fool Meade.

The Gettysburg campaign was over. Combined Union and Confederate losses totaled more than 50,000. The war would continue for almost two more years, but never again would Southern troops seriously threaten Northern soil.

Lee's engineers managed to erect a bridge across the Potomac before Meade arrived at Williamsport. The Confederates crossed over the hastily built bridge on the night of July 13, as shown in this painting (right). "We had them in our grasp," Lincoln said angrily when he heard of Lee's escape. "We had only to stretch our hands and they were ours."

This painting (below) shows the Army of Northern Virginia camped around Hagers- town, Maryland, waiting for the rain- swollen Potomac River to recede. Lee had originally hoped to cross the river at Harpers Ferry, Virginia, where there was a bridge. On July 3, however, Union cavalry overwhelmed the small force Lee had left behind to guard the crossing and destroyed the bridge. Lee was forced to move his exhausted army to Williamsport, Maryland.

LINCOLN'S GETTYSBURG ADDRESS

In August 1863, the governments of nineteen Union states contributed funds to buy a seventeen-acre plot at Gettysburg. The land would serve as a place of burial for the Northern soldiers who had fallen in the battle. Pennsylvania governor Andrew Curtin planned a special ceremony to commemorate this National Cemetery on November 19. The key speaker would be Edward Everett, a famous orator and former governor of Massachusetts. Curtin also invited Abraham Lincoln to offer "a few appropriate remarks."

After a two-hour speech by Everett, Lincoln spoke for less than two minutes. His message was simple. The men who had fallen at Gettysburg, said Lincoln, had died to give the nation "a new birth of freedom." In remembrance of their "last full measure of devotion," it was up to the living to finish the task the dead had begun, to ensure " . . . that government of the people, by the people, for the people, shall not perish from the earth."

There was little applause as the president sat down. "It is a flat failure and the people are disappointed," Lincoln remarked to his friend Ward Lamon. Most Northern newspapers agreed with him; one called the speech "silly, flat, and dishwatery." Yet some people recognized that Lincoln's short, simple speech had captured the essence of the great struggle consuming the divided nation.

Contrary to a popular story, Lincoln did not write his speech on the back of an envelope while traveling to the ceremony. The president wrote it in Washington, and although it totaled only about 270 words, the speech went through several drafts before he was satisfied. Lincoln did, however, revise the address slightly while on the train to Gettysburg. Shown here (opposite, top) is a draft in Lincoln's own handwriting.

Most of the audience at Gettysburg expected Lincoln to speak for more than two minutes, so a local photographer took his time setting up his bulky camera on its tripod. By the time he was ready to take the photograph, Lincoln had finished his address and was on his way back to his seat. According to one account of the ceremony, the audience, shown in this photograph, seemed more interested in watching the photographer prepare his equipment than in listening to the president.

Four score and seven years ago our fathers brought forth, upon this continent, a new nation, conceived in Liberty, and dedicated to the proposition that all men are created equal.

Now we are engaged in a great civil war, testing whether that nation, or any nation, so conceived, and so dedicated, can long endure. We are met here on a great battle-field of that war. We have come to dedicate a portion of it, as the final resting place for those who here gave their lives, that that nation might live. It is altogether fitting and proper that we should do this.

But in a larger sense we can not dedicate— we can not consecrate— we can not hallow this ground. The brave men, living and dead, who strug-

-gled here, have consecrated it far above our poor power to add or detract. The world will little note, nor long remember, what we say here, but can never forget what they did here. It is for us, the living, rather to be dedicated here to the unfinished work, which they have, thus far, so nobly carried on. It is rather for us to be here dedicated to the great task remaining before us— that from these honored dead we take increased devotion to that cause for which they here gave the last full measure of devotion— that we here highly resolve that these dead shall not have died in vain; that this nation shall have a new birth of freedom; and that this government of the people, by the people, for the people, shall not perish from the earth.

THE SIEGE OF VICKSBURG ENDS

"We certainly are in a critical situation," wrote a Southern doctor trapped in Vicksburg in June 1863, "but we can hold out until Johnston arrives with reinforcements and attacks the Yankees . . . [President] Davis can't intend to sacrifice us."

The Confederate president desperately wanted to hold the important port at Vicksburg, but there were simply no troops to send. In the East, all available soldiers were on their way to Gettysburg with Lee. In the West, William Rosecrans's Union forces blocked any movement by Braxton Bragg's Army of Tennessee. Confederate general Joseph Johnston considered Vicksburg "hopeless," and made only a weak movement toward the besieged city.

On June 28, Confederate general Pemberton received a letter signed simply "many soldiers." It read, "If you can't feed us, you had better surrender us, horrible as the idea is, than suffer this noble army to disgrace itself by desertion . . . This army is now ripe for mutiny, unless it can be fed." Pemberton considered an escape to the western bank of the Mississippi, but Union gunboats blocked the way. When he questioned his officers about the possibility of a breakout through Grant's lines, they told him flatly that such a move was impossible. On July 3, after six weeks of siege, Pemberton sent a messenger out with a white flag to ask Grant for surrender terms.

With a Confederate flag flying defiantly over the city, Union troops prepare for the siege of Vicksburg. The officer with the field glasses (lower right) in this lithograph (opposite, top) by Kurz & Allison may be General Grant. "The fall of Vicksburg and the capture of most of the garrison can only be a matter of time," wrote Grant to Union general in chief Henry W. Halleck as his 71,000 soldiers dug in.

This photograph (right) shows Union dugouts on a Vicksburg hillside, part of a line that eventually stretched fifteen miles. At some points the Union and Confederate trenches practically touched. An Iowa officer wrote that "our lines were so close together that our pickets [sentries] often had a cup of coffee or a chew of tobacco with the Rebel pickets at night." Once the conversation turned to politics, the soldiers of the opposing armies broke off their conversation "to avoid a fight on the subject."

THE FALL OF VICKSBURG

Pemberton's request came around the same time that Pickett's men were beginning their charge up Cemetery Hill in far-off Gettysburg. The people at Vicksburg soon learned that Grant wanted the surrender terms signed on the Fourth of July. Some of Pemberton's officers questioned the wisdom of surrendering on a day that meant so much to the men of both armies. Pemberton replied, "As a Northern man, I know that we can get better terms from them on the Fourth of July than on any other date of the year."

Grant at first demanded unconditional surrender. When Pemberton threatened to break off negotiations, however, Grant modified his stand. Realizing that shipping 30,000 Confederates to prison camps in the North would place a heavy burden on his transportation system, he agreed to parole the Confederate garrison. Under the parole system, the Confederates would be allowed to return to their homes after swearing not to fight for the Confederacy until they were officially exchanged for Union prisoners in the South. Pemberton approved Grant's offer, and on July 4 Grant and his army entered Vicksburg.

The Union soldiers didn't behave like conquerors. They greeted their former enemies with friendly shouts and shared their rations with hungry Southern soldiers and civilians. Grant later wrote, "I myself saw our men taking bread from their haversacks and giving it to the enemy they had been so recently engaged in starving out."

The hungry people of Vicksburg watch as Grant's men enter the city on July 4 (opposite, top); their parade was a combined victory and Independence Day celebration. "Bands were playing, troops were marching to and fro through the streets, and the cannon opened the national salute at noon, which was kept up by gunboats until after 2 o'clock p.m.," wrote one of Vicksburg's citizens.

Calmly smoking his ever-present cigar, Grant meets Pemberton on the steps of the Vicksburg courthouse following the city's fall. Like many officers on opposing sides in the Civil War, Grant and Pemberton had been friends in the "Old Army." When General Winfield Scott had officially praised Lieutenant Grant's bravery during the Mexican War, it was Lieutenant Pemberton who had brought Grant the good news.

THE FALL OF PORT HUDSON

The fall of Vicksburg was a triumph for the Union. Coming on the heels of Lee's defeat at Gettysburg, it greatly raised morale in the North. It split the South vertically, isolating the eastern part of the Confederacy from the resources of West. The victory also established Ulysses S. Grant as the Union's foremost general. Hearing news of the city's capture, a jubilant Lincoln shouted, "Grant is my man, and I am his for the rest of the war!"

Despite the loss of Vicksburg, the Confederacy still held one major Mississippi River stronghold—Port Hudson, Louisiana. As at Vicksburg, a formidable network of natural and manmade defenses protected Port Hudson.

The siege of Port Hudson began at the end of May. General Nathaniel Banks commanded the 20,000 Union soldiers outside the city. Like Grant at Vicksburg, Banks first tried to take Port Hudson by a direct assault, but the Northerners were thrown back with heavy casualties and settled down to a siege.

The 7,000 Confederates in Port Hudson hoped that Joseph Johnston would drive off Banks after defeating Grant at Vicksburg. When the news came that Vicksburg had fallen, the garrison at Port Hudson surrendered on July 9. The Union now had full control of the Mississippi River.

Confederate general Franklin Gardner surrendered Port Hudson to Union general Banks on July 9, 1863 (right), five days after the fall of Vicksburg. The siege cost the Union 3,000 casualties, the Confederates 7,200 (which included 5,500 troops taken prisoner). The capture of Port Hudson marked the beginning of full Union control of the Mississippi River.

The siege of Port Hudson, wrote a participant, was "forty days and nights in the wilderness of death." Union general Nathaniel Banks—who owed his rank to political influence, not military skill—first tried to capture the city with an infantry assault. A scornful Union officer commented that Banks ordered the attack "in the hope that some stroke of luck might give him the victory." Confederate defenders bombard Union ships in the port in this Prang lithograph (below).

THE BATTLE OF CHICKAMAUGA

While Grant besieged Vicksburg and Lee prepared to invade the North, Union general William Rosecrans finally began moving through Tennessee. His goal was Chattanooga on the Tennessee River. The city's capture would cut the eastern Confederacy's rail links with the West. Control of Chattanooga would also open the way for a Union advance into the heart of the Confederacy by way of Georgia.

In August, Rosecrans surrounded Chattanooga, and the overly cautious Bragg decided to evacuate it and retreat into Georgia. Union troops entered Chattanooga on September 9.

Rosecrans moved confidently into Georgia to finish off Bragg—but he was marching into a trap. Jefferson Davis had rushed reinforcements west, including James Longstreet's veterans from the Army of Northern Virginia. At dawn on September 19, Union and Confederate patrols clashed near Chickamauga Creek in the opening skirmishes of one of the war's bloodiest battles.

Some said Chickamauga meant "river of death" in the Cherokee Indian language. All day, Union and Confederate forces fought savagely, sometimes hand-to-hand. As darkness fell, most of the Union Army, including Rosecrans, retreated back toward Chattanooga. One corps under Virginia-born George Thomas held their ground, allowing their retreating comrades to get away safely. Thomas won the nickname "Rock of Chickamauga" for his gallant stand.

John Bell Hood (1831–79; left), leader of the Confederacy's famed "Texas Brigade," lost a leg at Chickamauga. He had already lost the use of his arm at Gettysburg, but even these two severe wounds couldn't keep "the Gallant Hood" out of action. In later campaigns, he rode into battle strapped to his horse. Although Hood's tough Texans loved him—they chanted his name as they attacked at Chickamauga—he would later prove too reckless for high command.

By the time A. R. Waud sketched this view (below) of Union troops moving up to the fighting at Chickamauga, the dead and wounded of both sides practically covered the ground. "The dead were piled upon each other . . . like cord wood, to make passage for the advancing columns," wrote a Union officer on the scene. "The sluggish stream of Chickamauga ran red with human blood."

THE CHATTANOOGA CAMPAIGN

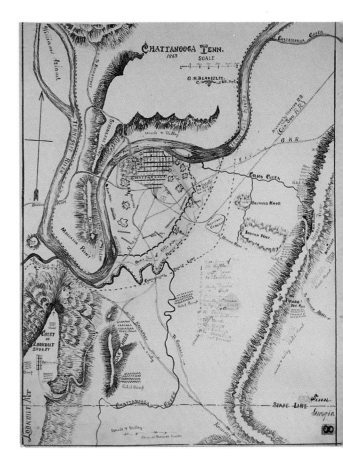

The fighting at Chickamauga continued throughout the following day. Despite the Confederate victory, Bragg and Longstreet failed to destroy Thomas's corps and the other Union troops still on the battlefield. The Northerners finally withdrew toward Chattanooga under cover of darkness. About 35,000 men on both sides had been killed, wounded, or captured during the two-day battle. Bragg, shocked by the heavy casualties, chose not to follow up with an attack on the retreating Union troops. Instead, he surrounded the city and prepared to starve the Northerners into surrender.

The Northern defeat at Chickamauga—and the possibility that Chattanooga might be retaken by the Confederacy—spurred the Union high command into action. Reinforcements were rushed to Tennessee. Lincoln, believing that Rosecrans had acted "like a duck struck on the head," relieved him of command, replacing him with George Thomas. Next, the president put Grant in command of all Union operations between the Mississippi and the Appalachians.

Grant arrived outside Chattanooga on October 23. His first task was to open a supply line through the rugged Cumberland Mountains to get food and ammunition into Chattanooga. Soon this "cracker line" ended fears of starvation in the besieged city. By mid-November, Grant felt strong enough to attack the Confederate defenses surrounding Chattanooga.

This map (above) shows the city of Chattanooga lying within a bend in the Tennessee River. Behind the northern bank of the river lay the Cumberland Mountains; outside of the city was the Confederate-held high ground. The Union troops in Chattanooga were trapped. Unable to retreat over the mountains, their only way out of the city was through the Confederate lines.

The railroad in this lithograph (right), which depicts Lookout Mountain near Chattanooga, played an important role in the campaign for the city. By pulling together trains from all over the North, Secretary of War Edwin Stanton was able to send 20,000 men from the Army of the Potomac, with all their artillery and supplies, to reinforce Grant. The operation, completed in eleven days, was the largest, fastest military movement before the twentieth century.

THE BATTLE OF LOOKOUT MOUNTAIN

The Confederate line around Chattanooga ran in a rough semicircle. The key points in this line were two pieces of high ground—Missionary Ridge to the east and south and Lookout Mountain to the west.

Grant and Thomas decided to drive the Confederates off Lookout Mountain first. They expected a tough fight, but the Confederate positions were only thinly held. Bragg seemed unaware of the danger from the growing Union forces around Chattanooga. Instead of strengthening his lines, he sent Longstreet and 12,000 men away from Chattanooga in an attempt to recapture Knoxville, Tennessee, from a Northern force led by Ambrose Burnside. When the assault on Lookout Mountain began on November 24, the Union attackers outnumbered the defenders by about five to one.

Even though Southern resistance proved lighter than expected, it was still a spectacular fight. As the Union troops climbed up the steep, rocky slopes, fog drifted in, covering the mountain in a gray blanket. Gunfire flashed, in an observer's words, "like swarms of fire flies." Suddenly the fog lifted, and the troops watching below cheered as they saw the Union flag floating from the mountain's summit. Newspaper correspondents immediately dubbed the fight "the battle fought above the clouds."

This Kurz & Allison lithograph (right) depicts Union troops advancing up the fog-shrouded slopes of Lookout Mountain. Union casualties for the assault totaled less than 500 men. The Union victory had one unfortunate result: Most of the Confederate defenders escaped down the reverse slope of the mountain to strengthen the Southern line at nearby Missionary Ridge.

A Kentucky Union regiment raises the U.S. flag on the "steep, ragged, rocky" summit of Lookout Mountain in this lithograph (below). An eclipse of the moon took place on the night after the battle; some superstitious Southern troops viewed it as an omen of disaster.

MISSIONARY RIDGE

The attack on Missionary Ridge began at 4 p.m. on November 25. One Confederate force held a network of trenches and rifle pits at the base of the 500-foot-high ridge. Another was dug in on the summit. Grant, believing that an uphill assault would be suicidal, planned to take only the trenches at the ridge's base.

About 20,000 of George Thomas's troops charged the Confederate trenches. The Confederates at the base left their positions and raced uphill to join their comrades at the summit. Thomas's men seized the abandoned trenches, while Southerners rained bullets and cannonballs down on them from above.

The Northerners were in a bind. They weren't supposed to advance up the ridge, but they couldn't stay where they were. Suddenly, the Union soldiers swept forward, charging straight up the ridge. Grant, watching from nearby Orchard Knob, angrily asked his staff who had ordered the charge. No one, came the reply. General Gordon Granger said, "When those fellows get started, all hell can't stop them." When the Union troops reached the summit, the Confederates fled down the other side—one of the few times Southern troops panicked and ran from a battlefield.

The Union victory at Missionary Ridge ended the Chattanooga Campaign. The remainder of Bragg's beaten army retreated to Dalton, Georgia. After the disasters at Gettysburg and Vicksburg, the loss of Chattanooga deepened the South's gloom.

Union troops leap into the Confederate trenches along the top of Missionary Ridge in this dramatic Currier & Ives lithograph (right). The first regiment to reach the Southern line was the 24th Wisconsin; one of its officers, eighteen-year-old Captain Arthur MacArthur, planted the U.S. flag on the ridge's crest. MacArthur, who won the Medal of Honor for his feat, finished the war as a colonel and later became the father of General Douglas MacArthur.

Grant and Thomas watch as Union troops storm the trenches at the foot of Missionary Ridge in the distance—and continue up the slope without orders. Assistant Secretary of War Charles A. Dana, who also witnessed the brave but unauthorized assault, wrote to Lincoln, "The storming of the ridge by our troops was one of the greatest miracles of military history . . . The generals caught the inspiration of the men, and were ready themselves to undertake impossibilities."

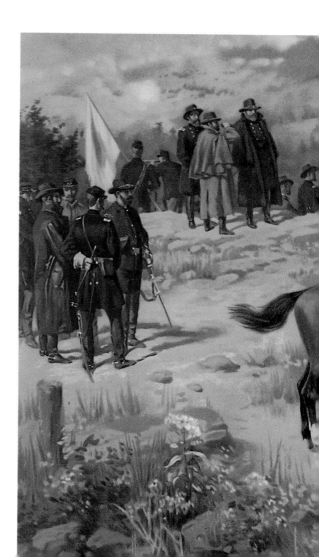

CHARLESTON

Throughout the summer of 1863, Union forces continued their campaign against Charleston, South Carolina. After the failed attack on Fort Wagner, the Union commander on land, General Quincy Gillmore, decided that artillery, not infantry, would have to do the job. He planned to shell Fort Wagner and nearby Fort Gregg into surrender, and to bombard Fort Sumter and the city of Charleston. Soon Union gunners were firing 5,000 shells a week at Sumter's thick brick walls.

To bombard Charleston, Gillmore stationed his troops on nearby Morris Island. He used one of the biggest guns the world had yet seen—a huge rifled cannon nicknamed "the swamp angel" because of Morris Island's marshy terrain. The swamp angel sent its first shell into Charleston on August 21. Two days later, after firing a total of thirty-six 200-pound shells, the swamp angel exploded. Despite Confederate protests about the "atrocity" of shelling a city full of civilians, damage and casualties were slight.

On September 7, Union troops again attacked forts Wagner and Gregg—only to find them abandoned. The way now seemed clear for Union gunboats to steam into Charleston Harbor. The Union naval commander, Rear Admiral John Dahlgren, wanted to make sure Fort Sumter was truly out of action before risking his ships. A small party of marines and sailors landed on the fort, only to be captured by 300 Confederates. Dahlgren called off the planned naval operation.

As 1863 ended, Charleston—the birthplace of secession—remained firmly in defiant Confederate hands.

Nonstop Union shelling in the summer of 1863 caused great damage to Fort Sumter, as shown in this painting (above). Although the bombardment of Charleston itself was not nearly this devastating, citizens were constantly aware of the Union gunners. Charleston resident Mary Chesnut calmly wrote in her diary, "It fairly makes me dizzy to think of that everlasting racket they are beating about people's ears."

The Currier & Ives lithograph shown here (right) depicts the fighting in Charleston Harbor in August 1863, the high point of the Union campaign to take the city. Northern mortars bombard forts Wagner and Gregg on Morris Island, while the gunboats of Admiral Dahlgren's fleet pound forts Sumter and Moultrie. At right is a cannon nicknamed the "swamp angel," lobbing one of its huge shells at Charleston.

Resource Guide

Key to picture positions: (T) top, (C) center, (B) bottom; and in combinations: (TL) top left, (TR) top right, (BL) bottom left, (BR) bottom right, (RC) right center, (LC) left center.

Key to picture locations within the Library of Congress collections (and where available, photo negative numbers): P - Prints and Photographs Division; R - Rare Book Division; G - General Collections; MSS - Manuscript Division; G&M - Geography Division

PICTURES IN THIS VOLUME

2–3 Little Round Top, P 4–5 flag, P 6–7 Lee, P 8–9 map, G

Timeline: 10–11 BL, Mud March, P, USZ62-173; TR, money, P, USZ62-40571 12–13 TL, immigrant, P; TR, Stephens, G; BR, battle, P, USZ62-14371 14–15 TL, Carson, P, USZ62-870; BL, battle, G; TR, Lincoln, P; BR, Morgan, P

Part I: 16–17 cavalry, P 18–19 TR, Lincoln, P; BR, cabinet, P, USA7-25808 20–21 TR, broadside, P, USZ62-950 22–23 TL, Thomas, P, B8172-6480; TR, Rosecrans, P; BR, gun crew, P, B811-2341 24–25 TR, Stones River, P; BR, reinforcements, G 26–27 BL, rifles, G; TR, railroad, P, USZ62-622; BR, telegraph, P, B8171-7117 28–29 TL, Porter, P; C, gunboats, P 30–31 TL, Farragut, P; TR, boat interior, G; BR, gunboat, G 32–33 TL, Grierson, G; TR, bridge, G; BR, crowd, G 34–35 TL, Johnston, P; C, battle, P, USZC4-1728 36–37 TL, Pemberton, P, USZ62-13286; C, digging, G 38–39 TR, troops, P, B8184-10358; C, gunboats, P 40–41 C, Ft. Wagner, P 42–43 TL, Hooker, P, BH8184-10366; C, Lee and Jackson, P, USZC4-995 44–45 TL, Jackson, G; C, battle, P 46–47 TL, stretcher bearers, G; C, dead, P, B8184-B605

48–49 TR, cavalry, G; C, Zouaves, P, B8171-7327 50–51 TL, Lee on horse, G; TR, Meade and staff, P, B8171-7330; BR, river, G

Part II: 52–53 Vicksburg, P 54–55 C, view, P 56–57 TL, Hill, P; BR, Buford and staff, P, B8184-4061 58–59 TL, Ewell, P; C, Louisiana Tigers, P 60–61 TL, Hancock, P; TR, dead, P, B8171-245 62–63 C, peach orchard, P 64–65 C, Little Round Top, P, USZ62-14374; BR, dead, P 66–67 BL, map, G&M; TR, Cemetery Hill (Forbes), P, USZC4-1005; BR, Waud, P 68–69 TR, Longstreet and Pickett, P, USZ62-043635; C, encampment, P, USZ62-14372 70–71 C, Pickett's Charge, P 72–73 C, pursuit, P 74–75 TR, Hagerstown, P, USZC4-975; C, escape, P, USZC4-979 76–77 TR, document, MSS; BR, crowd, P, B8184-10454 78–79 TR, Vicksburg, P; BR, dugouts, P, B8184-10608 80–81 TR, parade, G; BR, Grant and Pemberton, G 82–83 TR, surrender, P; C, Port Hudson, P 84–85 TL, Hood, P; C, battle, P, USZ62-7041 86–87 TL, map, G&M; TR, train, P, USZ62-1726 88–89 TR, flag, P, USZ62-15767; C, fog, P 90–91 TR, Missionary Ridge, P; C, Grant and Thomas, P 92–93 C, Fort Sumter, P; BR, Charleston Harbor, P

SUGGESTED READING

BATTY, PETER AND PETER PARISH. *The Divided Union.* Topsfield, Mass.: Salem House, 1987.

CATTON, BRUCE. *The American Heritage Picture History of the Civil War.* New York: Bonanza Books, 1982.

COFFEY, VINCENT J. *The Battle of Gettysburg.* Morristown, N. J.: Silver Burdett Company, 1985.

FOMER, ERIC AND OLIVIA MAHONEY. *A House Divided.* Chicago: Chicago Historical Society, 1990.

SMITH, CARTER. *The Civil War.* New York: Facts on File, 1989.

TIME-LIFE. *Brother Against Brother.* New York: Prentice Hall, 1990.

Index